PLAY THE PART

CHEF

Written by Liz Gogerly

Photographs by Chris Fairclough

WAYLAND

First published in 2011
by Wayland

Copyright © Wayland 2011

Wayland
338 Euston Road
London NW1 3BH

Wayland Australia
Level 17/207 Kent Street
Sydney, NSW 2000

Editors: Paul Humphrey, James Nixon
Design: D. R. ink
Commissioned photography: Chris Fairclough

Picture credits: Shutterstock: pp. 4 (Olly),
5 (Monkey Business Images), 6 left (Erwinova),
8 left (VR Photos), 10 (Corepics).

British Library Cataloguing in Publication Data
Gogerly, Liz.
    Chef. -- (Play the part)
    1. Cooks--Juvenile literature. 2. Cooks--Juvenile drama.
    3. Role playing--Juvenile literature.
    I. Title II. Series
    641.5'092-dc22

    ISBN: 978 0 7502 6509 6

Printed in China

Wayland is a division of Hachette Children's Books,
an Hachette UK Company

www.hachette.co.uk

The author, packager and publisher would like to thank
Davigdor Infants' School, Hove for their help and
participation in this book.

Contents

What is a chef?

A chef is a person who cooks for other people. Chefs work in the kitchens of schools, hospitals, cafes and restaurants – anywhere food is served. They cook all sorts of dishes from tasty pasta to delicious fish, and tempting ice creams to gorgeous cakes.

Chefs have long and busy working days. They start off by planning the menu for that day. Then they buy or order the food. Once chefs have everything they need, they begin to prepare the food. Finally, they cook and present the finished dishes for their customers.

What do chefs wear?

Most chefs wear a uniform. The jacket is made from thick white cotton. The tough material protects the chef from the hot oven and splashes of sizzling-hot food.

The jacket is white so it looks **hygienic** and clean. **Professional chefs** might also wear black and white checked trousers and a **necktie**. Most chefs wear a big white hat called a *toque*.

You can dress up as a chef wearing an old white shirt worn backwards. You can also buy a full chef costume at toyshops.

Make your own chef's hat

You will need:

★ White paper
★ Thin white card
★ Sticky tape
★ Scissors

1 Cut out a strip of white card to make a hatband. Measure the band around your head and cut the strip so there is 2 cm of card left at each end.

2 Cut out a sheet of white paper the same length as the card hatband.

3 Fold the paper into pleats. Each pleat should measure 2 cm.

4 To make the first pleat fold over the shorter edge of the paper about 2 cm.

5 To make the second pleat turn the paper over and fold the paper another 2 cm.

6 Repeat folding and turning over the paper until you reach the end of the paper.

7 Now join the ends of the paper with sticky tape to form a chef's hat shape.

8 Attach the hatband to the bottom of the hat with sticky tape.

The chef's kitchen

A chef's workplace is the kitchen. Chefs have lots of **kitchen utensils,** such as knives and spoons and pots and pans. They also have **electrical appliances,** such as **mixers** and **blenders**.

It's easy to set up your own chef's kitchen. You can use a toy oven or make a box into a pretend oven. There are lots of toy kitchen utensils that you can buy. Real pots and proper wooden spoons are great, too.

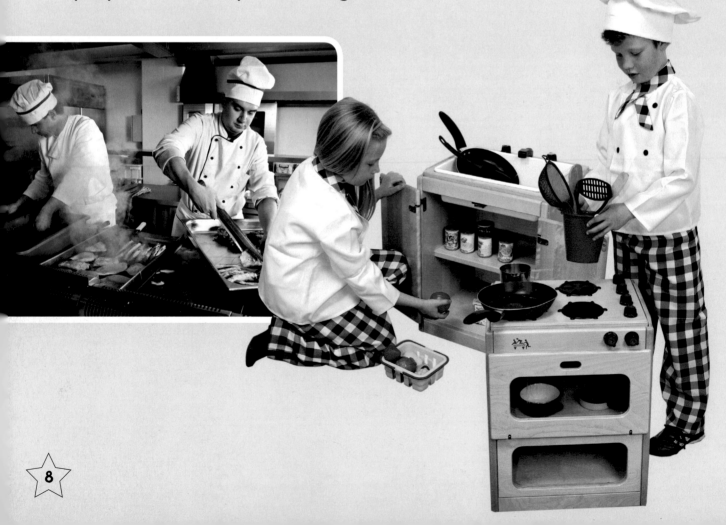

Make your own birthday cake

1 Paint the tin or container with white paint to make the base of the cake.

2 Write the words 'HAPPY BIRTHDAY' on the cake.

3 Decorate the cake with scrunched up tissue paper. Glue the tissue paper to the top of the cake.

You will need:

★ Round empty sweet tin or plastic container
★ White paint
★ Tissue paper
★ Real cake decorations (edible sugar sprinkles)
★ Birthday candles
★ Modelling clay
★ Felt-tip pen
★ Glue

4 Roll out two long pieces of modelling clay to make piping to go around the top and bottom of the cake.

5 Press the piping gently onto the edges of the cake to make it stick.

6 Add small balls of modelling clay to the top of the piping for more decoration.

7 To make candle holders, arrange some balls of modelling clay on top of the cake.

8 Press the birthday candles into the clay to make them stick.

9 Finish off by adding some real cake decorations. Put a few blobs of glue on top of the cake and cover with the edible sugar sprinkles.

Tasty food

Chefs are trained to cook up tasty meals. Lots of chefs try to make their meals healthy. They use fresh fruit and vegetables, which they buy from local markets or shops.

We need a balanced diet to grow, keep active and stay healthy. We should all eat at least five portions of fruit and vegetables every day!

Make your own pizza

You will need:
....
★ Thin yellow sponge cleaners
★ Red paint
★ Thin strips of yellow paper
★ Circles of white paper
★ Modelling clay
★ Glue
★ Scissors

1   Cut out a round pizza shape from the yellow sponge cleaners.

2   To make the tomato sauce topping for the pizza, cover one side of the pizza with red paint.

3   When the paint is dry you are ready to add the 'cheese' to the pizza. Glue strips of yellow paper and circles of white paper on top of the tomato sauce.

4   Use modelling clay to make vegetables like pepper, broccoli, mushrooms and sweetcorn.

5   Glue the vegetables on top of the pizza.

11

Create your own café

You can set up your own café or restaurant. First of all you need to think about what kind of café you would like to set up. Italian restaurants sell mostly pizza and pasta. Some cafés serve up tasty breakfasts.

Set up your own café

Arrange the tables with the chairs around them. You could put tablecloths, vases with flowers and napkins on the tables. Lay the cutlery and salt and pepper pots on each table. Remember to put a **menu** on each table, too.

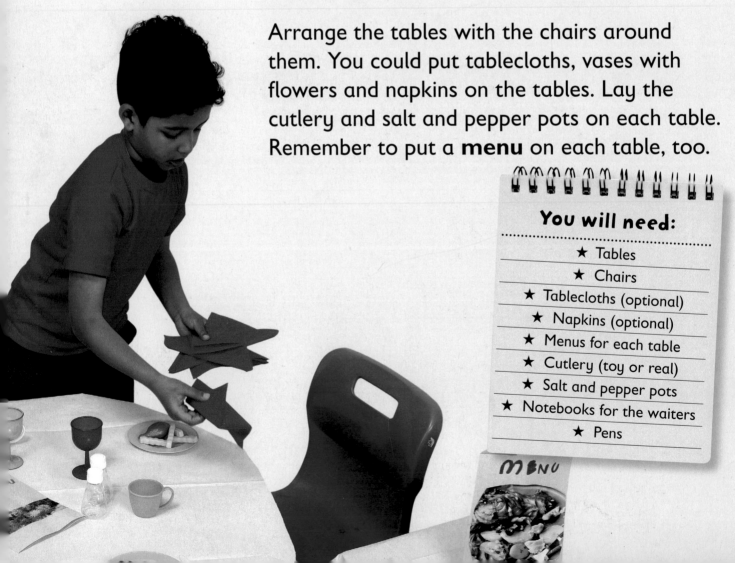

You will need:
- ★ Tables
- ★ Chairs
- ★ Tablecloths (optional)
- ★ Napkins (optional)
- ★ Menus for each table
- ★ Cutlery (toy or real)
- ★ Salt and pepper pots
- ★ Notebooks for the waiters
- ★ Pens

MENU

Make your own menu

You can write your own menu or a grown-up can help you make your menu on a computer.

MENU

STARTERS

Soup	£1.00
Garlic bread	£1.00
Pitta bread with dips	£1.50

MAIN COURSE

Sausages, mash and peas	£3.00
Pizza and salad	£2.50
Spaghetti Bolognese	£3.00
Macaroni cheese	£2.00
Tuna salad	£2.50
Beef burger in a bun	£2.00
Vegetable and cheese pie and chips	£3.0

PUDDING

MENU

DRINKS

Tea	... £1.00
Coffee	... £1.20
Hot chocolate	... £1.20
Orange juice	... £1.00
Apple juice	... £1.00
Lemonade	... £2.00
Sparkling Water	... £1.00

You have set the scene and made some props. Now you can begin to play the part of a chef in these role plays.

The best birthday cake ever!

Play the part of two busy chefs baking a birthday cake.

 CHEF 1: *(reading recipe book)* This is going to be the best birthday cake ever!

 CHEF 2: We'd better be quick – the party starts in two hours!

 CHEF 1: Right! Mix the butter with the sugar.

(Chef 2 pretends to stir the ingredients in a bowl.)

 CHEF 2: *(works quickly)* Done! What next?

CHEF 1: Mix in two eggs.

(Chef 1 pretends to break the eggs into the bowl.)

 CHEF 2: It's looking good. Now add the flour.

 CHEF 1: *(tastes the mixture)* Mmm, it needs something else... I'll add my secret **ingredient**. *(stirs in a few drops of **flavouring**)*

WHAT HAPPENS NEXT?

You can decide what happens next in this scene. Below are some fun ideas that you could try acting out using your own words. Then have a go at making up your own scenes.

1 Chef 1's 'secret ingredient' has made the cake taste horrible. She looks at the bottle to see what went wrong. She discovers she used hot chilli sauce!

2 The oven breaks down. The chefs rush out and buy a birthday cake from the shops instead.

3 The cake is perfect. The chefs decorate the cake. The customer says it's the best birthday cake ever!

The fruit salad story

Act out this scene set in a café. Play the parts of a customer, waiter and chef. You can use toy fruit or fruit made with modelling clay.

 WAITER: Hello. Are you ready to order yet?

 CUSTOMER: *(reading menu)* Mmm, I'd like something healthy please.

 WAITER: I'll ask the chef. *(waiter goes to the kitchen)*

 WAITER: The customer wants a healthy meal. Can you help?

 CHEF: I know! I'll make a delicious fruit salad.

 WAITER: *(waiter goes back to customer)* Would you like a fruit salad?

 CUSTOMER: Oh, yes please! But I'm in a rush so please be quick! *(waiter rushes back to the kitchen)*

 WAITER: Great! Please can we have the fruit salad.

 CHEF: *(starts to prepare the fruit salad)* No problem!

WHAT HAPPENS NEXT?

You can decide what happens next in this scene. Below are some fun ideas that you could try acting out using your own words. Then have a go at making up your own scenes.

1 The chef makes a terrible fruit salad. The customer sends it back to the kitchen. The diner has to choose another meal.

2 The chef takes too long making the fruit salad. The customer leaves without eating. The chef is upset.

3 The fruit salad is perfect. The customer gives the waiter a large **tip** when she pays.

Sizzling sausages!

In this scene you can play the parts of two chefs. Find out who makes the best breakfast in this fast and funny play.

 CHEF: *(looks at the order)* OK. It's another breakfast – sausages, fried eggs and toast.

 JUNIOR CHEF: Yes, chef!

 CHEF: OK, you do the eggs. I'll do the sausages and toast.

 JUNIOR CHEF: Yes, chef!
(pretends to break eggs into a frying pan)

 CHEF: *(drops sausages on the floor)* Oh bother! I better get some more.
(Chef starts cooking sausages in a frying pan.)

 JUNIOR CHEF: *(cooking the eggs)* The eggs are ready, chef.

 CHEF: Very good! I'll get the toast on!
(pops toast in the toaster)

JUNIOR CHEF: Oh dear chef, your sausages are burning!

 CHEF: Disaster! And, so is my toast. Everything is going wrong today!

 JUNIOR CHEF: Don't worry chef. We'll cook some perfect sizzling sausages in no time…

WHAT HAPPENS NEXT?

You can decide what happens next in this scene. Below are some fun ideas that you could try acting out using your own words. Then have a go at making up your own scenes.

1 The chef gets angry and storms off. The junior chef steps in and makes his own recipe of sizzling sausages, crispy bacon, delicious tomatoes and perfect eggs.

2 The chefs work as a team to make a lovely breakfast. The customer is very happy.

3 The chefs have run out of sausages. Quickly they decide what else they can make for their hungry customers.

Pizza or pie?

Play the parts of the customer, chef and waiter in this scene. Find out what happens when the orders get mixed up.

 WAITER: *(goes up to the customer waiting at table 1)* Good evening. Would you like a menu?

 CUSTOMER 1: Oh, yes. Thanks!

 WAITER: The pizza is very good tonight.

 CUSTOMER 1: *(looks at the menu)* Actually, I'd like a piece of pie, please.

 WAITER: Right away, sir.

(Waiter goes to the kitchen.)

 **WAITER:** *(shouts)* That'll be a piece of pie for table 1, chef!

 CHEF: Coming straight up!

CUSTOMER 2: *(calls to the waiter)* Excuse me, waiter. Please can I order?

WAITER: *(goes up to the customer waiting at table 2)* Good evening. What would you like?

CUSTOMER 2: Can I order a drink please?

WAITER: Certainly!

CUSTOMER 2: I'll have a hot chocolate please.

WAITER: *(waiter gives order to the chef)* A hot chocolate for table 2!

CHEF: Coming straight up!

(continued over page)

Pizza or pie?

(continued)

 WAITER: Do you have the order for table 1 yet?

 CHEF: *(gives the waiter a pizza)* Here you go. One of my best…

 WAITER: That's not a piece of pie.

 CHEF: *(shouts)* No, it's a pizza. You said pizza pie!

 WAITER: *(shouts)* No, I said piece of pie.

 CHEF: Oh dear!

 WAITER: And where is the hot chocolate?

 CHEF: *(shouts)* What hot chocolate? I made a hot chocolate pudding.

WAITER: *(shouts)* I said HOT CHOCOLATE!

 CUSTOMER 1: I don't think much of this place! Waiter, I'm leaving.

 CUSTOMER 2: All I wanted was a quiet drink – not all this shouting…

WHAT HAPPENS NEXT?

You can decide what happens next in this scene. Below are some fun ideas that you could try acting out using your own words. Then have a go at making up your own scenes.

1   The waiter and chef calm down. The waiter tells the customers they can have a free pudding if they wait a little longer for their orders. Everyone is happy.

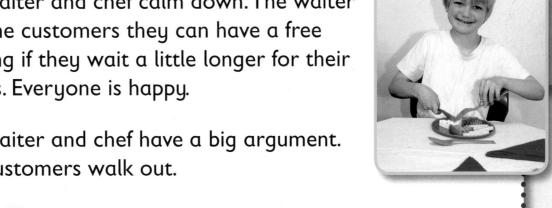

2   The waiter and chef have a big argument. The customers walk out.

3   The chef walks out! The waiter takes over in the kitchen and cooks a perfect piece of pie and an excellent hot chocolate. The customers give him a big tip!

GLOSSARY

blender An electric mixing machine that turns food into liquid.

electrical appliances Machines that need electricity to work.

flavouring An ingredient that can change the taste of food or drink.

hygienic Describes something that is clean and helps people to stay healthy.

ingredients The items of food and drink that are mixed together when food is prepared.

kitchen utensils Tools that are used for preparing food in the kitchen, such as knives, spoons, whisks and mashers.

menu A list of dishes and drinks available for a meal in a café or restaurant.

mixer An electric machine that mixes, beats, whips and whisks food together.

necktie A band of material that is worn around the neck and tied in a knot at the front.

professional chef A person that has been to catering college to learn how to cook food and has passed exams about cooking food.

tip A sum of money given to someone as a reward for doing a good job.

INDEX

Play the Part

Contents of books in the series:

WAYLAND